THE BIG BOOK OF FESTIVALS

THE BIG BOOK OF FESTIVALS

MARITA BULLOCK & JOAN-MAREE HARGREAVES Illustrated by LIZ ROWLAND

LOTHIAN

For Claude

*Many thanks to Jacquie Brown, Jeanmarie Morosin,
Kate Stevens, Liz Seymour and the Hachette team*

A Lothian Children's book
Published in Australia and New Zealand in 2021
by Hachette Australia
Level 17, 207 Kent Street, Sydney NSW 2000
www.hachettechildrens.com.au

The creators of this book acknowledge Australia's Aboriginal and Torres Strait Islander peoples, the Traditional Custodians of lands, waterways and skies across Australia.

A catalogue record for this book is available from the National Library of Australia

ISBN: 978 0 7344 1997 2 (hardback)

Cover and internal design by Seymour Designs
Colour reproduction by Splitting Image
Printed in Singapore

CONTENTS

Keep a lookout for these children enjoying their local festivals with their families!

INTRODUCTION

Tomato-throwing parties, graveside picnics, fire-walking ceremonies, crying baby competitions and the biggest bathing festival on Earth – this book introduces you to some of the world's most incredible cultural and religious festivals dating back hundreds, sometimes thousands of years.

Traditionally, festivals were held to mark significant events in the natural world such as changes in seasons, the beginning or ending of calendar years and harvest times. Festivals also developed to worship gods or powerful natural forces such as the sun, water or moon. Today, festivals reflect changes brought by modern life, and they continue to evolve as more people travel or move to new homes across the globe.

Some festivals are outrageously fun and joyful, with strong ties to cultural traditions and customs. Others are more serious in their commitment to the worship of a god, a spiritual being or a religious occasion. One of the wonderful things about all festivals is the way they bring people together as a community, enabling a break from everyday routines to celebrate important occasions and big events in life.

Countless festivals take place around the world each year, and if we had enough room to fit them all in this book, we would have! We've included some of the world's largest festivals, as well as smaller, regional festivals such as Valencia's La Tomatina, Queensland's Bunya Dreaming, Northern Greece's Anastenaria and Konya's Whirling Dervishes. There's also a section on festivals connected to the seasons, such as Iran's Nowruz and Japan's Hanami, and a collection of fantastic festivities and events that are unique to places ranging from Ireland and Spain to Bali and Taiwan.

The pages in this book are filled with the colourful symbols and motifs that mark these occasions – music, song, dance, food, family, friends, gifts, plants, flowers, games, candles and light. We hope you will be inspired to learn more about the different ways people celebrate around the world, and all of their diverse traditions, customs and beliefs.

There's so much to celebrate in this big wide world of ours, so let's get into it!

ANASTENARIA

MARVEL AT THIS INCREDIBLE FIRE-WALKING RITUAL IN NORTHERN GREECE

Could you walk barefoot across red-hot coals with temperatures of up to 400° Celsius? This is exactly what happens in parts of northern Greece during Anastenaria, an annual religious festival devoted to two Greek Orthodox saints. Devotees can walk barefoot over hot coals without the slightest trace of harm. Some describe this feat as a great mystery, but for the fire-walkers their ability to withstand fire is simple: they believe they are protected by the icons of saints Constantine and Helen, which they hold while walking over the burning coals.

The ritual takes place in the evening after hours of singing and dancing in the *konáki* – the special religious houses where the icons of saints Constantine and Helen are kept, and where people congregate before the fire-walk. The singing and dancing helps the fire-walkers achieve an altered state of consciousness. Many describe a feeling of 'being taken by the spirit'. Some dance on the coals in a trance-like state, while others run quickly across or dance dramatically in a state of ecstasy. Afterwards there is a traditional dance around the fire and more dancing in the *konáki* before a meal with family and friends.

WHERE AND WHEN The festival is celebrated by some Greek–Macedonian communities around Thessaloniki in northern Greece, and in parts of southern Bulgaria. Celebrations take place around 21 to 23 May and can last anywhere between three days and a week.

The music performed inside the *konáki* is Thracian folk music using a lyre, a drum and a piped instrument called a *ghaidha*.

Many legends exist about the ability to walk on fire. Some say Saint Constantine's enemies tried to burn him, but he remained unharmed due to his connection to God.

Mikháli has been helping his mother prepare for Anastenaria for months. They have candles, incense and oil to burn inside the *konáki*.

Music helps the fire-walkers to prepare for their walk over the hot coals.

Anastenarides believe if someone is burned by the fire they haven't been protected by the saints!

THE BIRTHDAY OF GURU NANAK

HONOUR THE BIRTHDAY OF ONE OF THE FOUNDING FATHERS OF SIKHISM

This day celebrates Guru Nanak as one of the ten gurus who founded the Sikh religion more than 500 years ago in India. The birthday of Guru Nanak is one of the most significant events for Sikhs.

The celebrations begin two days before Guru Nanak's actual birth date. On the first day, Sikh men and women read the holy book, the *Guru Granth Sahib*, aloud from beginning to end. Each person reads for two to three hours before the next person takes over. This ritual is called *Akhand Path*. On the second day, the holy book is paraded through the streets of Amritsar in an ornate hand-held carriage decorated with tassels. Five people dressed in orange and holding the Sikh flag lead the procession. On Guru Nanak's birthday, large processions start as soon as the sun rises. Musicians and singers chant hymns from the holy book. The procession ends with a prayer at a *gurdwara* (a sacred place of worship) in the evening.

WHERE AND WHEN Sikhs celebrate the birthday of Guru Nanak all over the world, with notable celebrations taking place in parts of India and Pakistan. The shrine Gurdwara Janam Asthan in Pakistan is a particularly important place where Sikhs gather. The birthday of Guru Nanak is celebrated on the full moon day of the month of Kartik, usually in November.

After prayers, Anu enjoys a vegetarian meal followed by a sweet dish called *karah parshad*, made from wheat flour, sugar and ghee. →

Sikhism is the world's fifth largest religion with around 25 million followers worldwide.

Sikhs often wear head coverings. Men traditionally wore turbans to protect their hair and keep it long; Sikhs believe hair is one of God's gifts and therefore it should not be cut. Women also wear scarves or turbans to protect their long hair.

The celebration of Guru Nanak's birthday has many names! It is sometimes called Guru Nanak Gurpurab, Guru Nanak's Prakash Utsav or Guru Nanak Dev Ji Jayanti.

BUDDHA DAY

CELEBRATE BUDDHA'S BIRTHDAY, THE MOST IMPORTANT DAY IN THE YEAR FOR MANY BUDDHISTS

Buddha Day is a Buddhist festival celebrating the birth of Prince Siddhartha Gautama, the founder of Buddhism, around 2500 years ago. Buddhists the world over commemorate the birth of Buddha, but the celebrations vary in name and in custom depending on the country and the form of Buddhism followed – whether it is the Theravada, Mahāyāna or Vajrayāna (sometimes known as Matrayāna) tradition. Despite differences in customs, all Buddhists are united by their worship of Buddha, their offerings to monks and their visits to local temples for services and teachings.

Pilgrimage to sacred sites is a key part of Buddha's birthday celebrations. In Western Tibet, Buddhists journey to Mount Kailash (known as the centre of the universe by some devotees) to walk more than 50 kilometres around the mountain in a single day, before tying prayer flags to a giant flagpole in the area.

In Indonesia, hundreds of pilgrims and saffron-robed monks celebrate 'Waisak Day' by making a pilgrimage from the Candi Mendut Temple in Java to the largest Buddhist temple in the world at Borobudur. Once there, the devotees circle a massive stone monument (constructed in the ninth century to represent the Buddhist cosmology) where they meditate, leave offerings and chant into the night, before releasing a thousand lanterns into the sky.

WHERE AND WHEN Buddha's birthday is celebrated in countries around the world with Buddhist communities. It is a prominent festival throughout Asia, observed in countries including Taiwan, Japan, Cambodia, Laos, China, Hong Kong, India, Indonesia, Malaysia, Burma, Mongolia, Tibet, Nepal, North Korea, South Korea, Singapore, Thailand and Vietnam. The exact date for the celebration varies from year to year, depending on the Asian lunisolar calendar. Most celebrations usually fall in April or May (or occasionally June) in the Western (Gregorian) calendar, depending also on the year and location of the celebration.

Siddhartha Gautama was born between 563 and 480 BCE in Nepal's famous Lumbini Gardens.

In Seoul, Bae joins the 'Lotus Lantern Festival', where she walks with more than 100 000 pilgrims in *hanbok* dress through the streets. A street vendor helps her make a rainbow-coloured lantern in the shape of a tiger, which she carries to Jogyesa temple.

BUNYA DREAMING

CELEBRATE THE ANCIENT ABORIGINAL GATHERING IN HONOUR OF BONYI BURU, A VERY LARGE BUNYA NUT

Bunya gatherings have been occurring in Queensland, Australia, for thousands of years. In ancient times, Australia's first people gathered every two to three years to celebrate the harvest of bunya cones from the bunya tree. Mobs (Aboriginal clan groups) from areas as far afield as Victoria and Western Australia would travel to the Bunya Mountains and Blackall Ranges region of the Sunshine Coast for cultural ceremonies. At these gatherings, thousands of people performed cultural practices including corroborees, sharing song lines, trading tools, rare stones and traditional knowledge, and arranging of marriages. Issues of lore (law) were resolved off the mountain in a great plain near Dalby while families feasted on the bunya nuts they harvested in abundance.

The traditional gatherings ended around 1902, after English colonisation. Many Aboriginal people were taken to missions, and others were unable to follow their pathways to the Bunya Mountains due to fences. Bunya trees were also cut down for timber, displacing Indigenous communities and suppressing Indigenous cultures.

Despite these obstacles, Aboriginal people continued to harvest the bunyas every year, and in 2007, the bunya nut festival was reimagined as Bunya Dreaming. It attracts hundreds of Indigenous and non-Indigenous locals, who come together with the bunya trees along the rivers of the Sunshine Coast hinterland. The event is not an attempt to recreate a traditional gathering, but to reconnect the traditional practices and cultural knowledge with a modern twist.

WHERE AND WHEN Bunya Dreaming is held on Queensland's Sunshine Coast on 26 January when the bunyas are in full fruit and ripe for sharing.

The *bonyi* ('bunya pine' in the Gubbi Gubbi language) can live for about 600 years and can grow up to 50 metres high.

Today, Bunya Dreaming is just one of many contemporary festivals that celebrate traditional Indigenous culture around Australia. Other big festivals include the Garma Festival of Traditional Cultures and the Laura Aboriginal Dance Festival.

The nuts on the tree can weigh up to 10 kilograms – watch your head!

CARNAVAL

DANCE, SING AND PARTY AT ONE OF THE WORLD'S MOST SPECTACULAR STREET PARADES

Big feathered headdresses, colourful boas and sequins are on display at one of the biggest and greatest parties in the world: Rio de Janeiro's famous Carnaval. Each year, people flock to Rio to see spectacular parades filled with giant floats and elaborate costumes and to experience the rhythmic beats of samba – a traditional style of music and dance in Brazil.

Rio's Carnaval started around 200 years ago as a series of vibrant street parties, which emerged from different cultures and traditions. The Roman Catholic tradition of celebrating before Lent (the period of fasting before Easter) was brought to Brazil by Spanish and Portuguese colonists in the 1500s, along with their fancy pre-Lent masquerade balls, which contributed to the glitz and glamour of the early street parades.

Carnaval also has cultural influences from West Africa. Samba music and dance was introduced by the descendants of West African people, who were brought to Brazil as slaves by Spanish and Portuguese colonists between the 1500s and the 1800s.

WHERE AND WHEN Carnaval usually occurs in February or March for around five days before Lent. There are also smaller celebrations held in cities throughout Brazil and in other countries around the world.

Juliana will take part in the parade as one of the many drummers, providing the beats for the samba dancers.

Up to 1.5 million people visit Carnaval every year.

Nudity is not allowed in Carnaval, but this doesn't stop many of the dancers wearing very little! Nakedness symbolises a momentary abandonment of authority and rules.

A highlight of Carnaval is the spectacular samba competition that takes place between hundreds of different schools of samba dancers. Each samba school can have thousands of members, which makes the samba parades enormous events.

CARNEVALE DI VENEZIA

DAZZLE AT A MASQUERADE BALL DURING VENICE'S WORLD-FAMOUS CARNIVAL

Venice is famous around the world for its spectacular Carnevale celebrations. For around two weeks in the lead-up to Lent, the traditional Catholic period of fasting and restraint, Venice is filled with joyous abandon. People wear extravagant costumes and dazzling face masks at street parties and masquerade balls in palazzos (palaces) around the city.

The Venice carnival became famous for its glamorous parties and masquerade balls hundreds of years ago, when people wore masks to disguise their identity while indulging their senses in hedonistic pleasure. Strict laws designed to limit consumption, luxury and extravagance were relaxed during Carnevale, and this contributed to the atmosphere of carefree jubilance. Wearing masks also meant people could temporarily escape the social class they belonged to. No one could tell who was rich or poor, giving Venetians a freedom they didn't have throughout the year.

The carnival's atmosphere of social freedom meant it also became associated with danger and risk, and it was officially banned for almost 200 years by various rulers until it was resurrected by the Italian government in 1979.

WHERE AND WHEN Carnevale takes place in Venice's streets, in public places and in private palazzos throughout the city during the two weeks leading up to Shrove Tuesday, which marks the beginning of the Christian observance of Lent.

Carnevale is a time to let loose and rejoice in the relaxation of rules.

The origins of Carnevale are not known. Some historians date the festival back to the 11th century, after the Venice Republic celebrated its victorious battle against another Italian city, Aquileia.

Venetian masks were traditionally made out of glass, porcelain or leather. Many masks were decorated with paint, gold leaf, feathers and gems.

One of the most important events is the contest for the most beautiful mask, which is judged by a panel of international costume and fashion designers.

Matteo buys a mask to decorate with feathers, glitter and shiny paint.

CHRISTMAS

GATHER WITH FAMILY AND FRIENDS, AND SPREAD PEACE AND GOODWILL TO ALL PEOPLE ON EARTH

Christmas marks the birth of Jesus Christ more than 2000 years ago. It is a time of great celebration for Christians around the world because they believe that Christ's birth was a miracle crafted by God to spread peace on Earth.

Christ was born in Bethlehem to his father, Joseph, and his mother, Mary, in a stable surrounded by animals. Today, thousands of pilgrims and tourists visit the Church of the Nativity in Bethlehem, where it is believed Jesus was born.

WHERE AND WHEN While Christmas is celebrated worldwide in countries with Christian populations, people of different religions and people without religion often join in the celebrations too. In Bethlehem the celebrations continue right up until 18 January.

What has the birth of Christ got to do with Christmas trees, pudding and presents? Well, in Europe, the celebration of the birth of Christ overlapped with Europe's traditional midwinter festivities celebrating the end of the shortest and darkest day of the year, and the arrival of spring. Various customs such as gift-giving, parties, candles and fires marked the turning of the seasons, and the decoration of houses with plants such as holly and ivy were celebrated as emblems of ongoing life.

Christmas foods have changed over time. Turkey was only introduced as a Christmas dish in Britain in 1542, and it was not very popular until much later. In earlier times, wealthy people ate venison, boar's head or even swans and peacocks! Today, some Australians like to eat seafood on Christmas day because it is delicious in a summer climate.

Santa Claus takes on different guises in different countries. In France, he is known as Papa Noël, and in Russia and the Ukraine he is sometimes known as Father Frost.

Christmas foods and traditions have changed over time.

Anouk leaves a letter for Santa Claus under the Christmas tree, along with some milk and carrots for Santa's reindeers.

DÍA DE MUERTOS

DANCE TO AWAKEN THE SPIRITS AT MEXICO'S COLOURFUL PARTY FOR THE DEAD!

If you think death is a gloomy subject, think again! Día de Muertos, or Day of the Dead, is one of the most joyous and colourful celebrations in Mexico's annual calendar. Lasting for two days, Día de Muertos is an important time for families to celebrate and honour their dead. People wear makeup and costumes related to death, sing and dance, and make offerings to lost loved ones, whose spirits are believed to awaken for the parades and parties. The celebrations often take a humorous tone as Mexicans remember funny events and stories about the departed as a way to show their love and respect.

The first day of the celebrations, All Saints Day, is devoted to children who have died. The second day, All Souls Day, honours adults who have passed away. Families go to cemeteries to clean and visit the graves of their relatives, often spending all night at the gravesite, picnicking and celebrating by candlelight.

Colourful skulls called *calaveras* are made out of sugar, chocolate or papier-mâché.

WHERE AND WHEN Día de Muertos is celebrated throughout Mexico and in other parts of the world with large Mexican populations. It falls between 1 and 2 November each year.

Taste the candied pumpkin and sweet egg bread made into animal skeleton shapes.

La Catrina (Lady of the Dead) has become an icon of Día de Muertos.

Día de Muertos began several thousand years ago with the Aztec, Toltec, and other Nahua people, who considered mourning the dead disrespectful.

Brightly coloured altars or shrines are placed in homes, gravesites and public places to honour the dead, and encourage the souls of those departed to return. These altars are decorated with photographs of the person who has died and offerings of food, candles, tequila or special objects the person once enjoyed.

The Aztec marigold is a native Mexican flower, and it is used throughout the celebrations.

DIWALI

SHINE BRIGHTLY AT INDIA'S FESTIVAL OF LIGHT

Rooftops, houses, temples, streets, homes and rivers – everywhere radiates with light, joy and happiness. This is Diwali, the festival of lights, India's biggest and most important holiday, marking the beginning of the Hindu new year and the beginning of winter.

Diwali lasts for five days. The third day is the most important of the festival, with people placing tiny *diyas* (clay oil lamps), candles and electric lights around their houses. These lights symbolise the Hindu belief in the victory of light over darkness, knowledge over ignorance and good over evil. Families come together to pray and feast, exchanging gifts and bursting crackers.

WHERE AND WHEN Diwali is celebrated by Hindus, Sikhs and Jains across India, and in other countries where these communities live. The festival is particularly magnificent in India's ancient capital city of New Delhi. Some of the largest Diwali celebrations outside of India occur in the United Kingdom.

The date of Diwali changes each year, according to the position of the moon. It usually occurs between late October and mid-November.

Vedhika and Ayaan ⟶ light *diyas*, thought to help guide the goddess Lakshmi into people's homes, bringing fortune and luck.

The word 'Diwali' means 'row of lights'.

People gather to enjoy colourful sweets called *mithai*, dressed up in their finest clothes.

Faithful Hindus visit temples to offer *puja* (worship) and make offerings of fruit and sweets.

Rangoli patterns, made out of flower petals, coloured rice, sand or flour, decorate the ground outside temples and on the floors of houses. This is to attract Lakshmi, in the hope that she will bring good luck and prosperity in the new year.

EASTER

CELEBRATE NEW LIFE AND NEW BEGINNINGS ON ONE OF THE HOLIEST DAYS IN THE CHRISTIAN CALENDAR

Easter marks the anniversary of Jesus Christ's resurrection more than 2000 years ago. Christians believe that Christ was betrayed by Judas, one of his twelve disciples, and was nailed to a wooden cross in Jerusalem. Christ eventually died on the cross and was buried in a cave, but he came back to life three days later and remained on Earth for another 40 days and 40 nights.

There are many days of religious worship commemorating these events, including Palm Sunday (marking the beginning of Christ's last week on Earth); Maundy or Holy Thursday (commemorating his last supper); Good Friday (the anniversary of his crucifixion); and Easter Saturday (commemorating the period during which he lay in the tomb). Easter Sunday is the most important day of celebration, marking Christ's resurrection and the celebration of new life. Church services are held and hymns are sung. Masses sometimes take place at midnight or at dawn.

WHERE AND WHEN Easter is celebrated by Christians of all denominations around the world. It falls between 22 March and 25 April, on the first full moon (this marks the beginning of spring in the northern hemisphere).

Christ's resurrection is often celebrated with symbols of new life, such as eggs, baby chickens and rabbits.

Myra searches her garden for chocolate Easter eggs hidden by the Easter bunny.

Hot cross buns are traditionally eaten on Good Friday. The cross on top of the bun symbolises Christ's crucifixion.

The custom of giving eggs is an ancient one. In many places around the world, eggs made of chocolate wrapped in brightly coloured foil are given as gifts. In Russia and Poland, traditional wax-covered eggs are painted with elaborate and brightly coloured patterns.

In Switzerland, Easter eggs are delivered by a cuckoo and in parts of Germany by a fox!

EID UL-FITR

BREAK THE FAST AND CELEBRATE PEACE AND FORGIVENESS

The taste of food after fasting for a month is one of the great joys of Eid ul-Fitr, also sometimes known as Sweet Eid. Eid ul-Fitr is a special day celebrated by Muslims around the world to mark the end of the holy month of Ramadan. During Ramadan, Muslims abstain from eating during the day to show their devotion to Allah (God).

Eid ul-Fitr is celebrated with a large feast shared between family and friends. While Eid ul-Fitr means the 'festival of the breaking of the fast', it is not just an occasion of joyful eating – it is also an important day for Muslims to give thanks to Allah for his countless gifts.

WHERE AND WHEN Eid ul-Fitr is celebrated in many countries at the end of Ramadan, which takes place in the ninth month of the Islamic calendar. The date it occurs in the Western (Gregorian) calendar is different every year because the Western calendar is around eleven days longer than the Islamic calendar. The exact date may also vary from country to country depending on whether or not the moon has been sighted.

Muslims celebrate Eid ul-Fitr with an early morning visit to a mosque. They must wash before entering as a sign of respect for Allah. Special prayers are said and the day is spent praising Allah.

Kareem wishes his grandfather *Eid Mubarak* (a Blessed Eid) and offers him a *ma'amoul*, a small round pastry filled with dates, figs and walnuts.

Muslims give food to those who are poor and in need during Eid ul-Fitr.

Breakfast can include a bowl of *sheer khurma*, which is vermicelli and sweet milk with dates, raisins and nuts.

In some countries such as Egypt, Eid ul-Fitr lasts up to three days.

FESTIVAL OF GIANTS

SEE A CITY'S TALL TALES COME TO LIFE IN FRANCE AND BELGIUM'S GIANT CELEBRATION

Across Belgium and France each year, thousands of traditional characters from stories and legends take on larger-than-life proportions, appearing as giant papier-mâché figures paraded through the streets of villages and towns. This tradition started around 500 years ago, when religious leaders decided that the best way to educate ordinary people about religious matters was to tell important stories with giant characters. The idea took hold and the tradition continued throughout Belgium and France. Today, the parades feature all kinds of giants, including more contemporary figures. The performances vary from place to place, but the giants usually relate to the history, legend or life of the town. Music, singing and dancing accompany the parades and their re-enactments of legends and stories.

One of the most famous processions of giants happens in Ath, a small town in Belgium. This *ducasse* (procession) uses giants to enact a confrontation between the Biblical figures David and Goliath. The festival reinterprets scenes from this story, in which an ordinary shepherd boy, David, armed only with a sling and five stones, fights and kills the giant warrior Goliath.

One of the most famous giants in France is Monsieur Gayant, who is paraded alongside his wife, Madame Gayant, and their three children in the town of Douai. Monsieur Gayant is the tallest in France. He is 8.5 metres tall and weighs 350 kilograms.

WHERE AND WHEN The parades of giants happen in various towns in France and Belgium, including Douai and Ath. They usually take place around the end of July and the beginning of August.

The giants are so important in France they are almost treated as if they are real people! Townships sometimes stage weddings for the giants, or if a new giant is made it may be blessed with a christening ceremony.

Belgium has the largest giant in Europe, Jean Turpin of Nieuwpoort, which exceeds 11 metres.

Claude waits to catch the *gayantines* (lollies) thrown out to the crowd in Douai.

GELEDE

SING, DANCE, DRUM AND PAY TRIBUTE TO THE POWER OF MOTHERS

Gelede celebrates the power and spiritual role of women as bearers of life. It is a fun, light-hearted event that celebrates all mothers in the Yoruba communities in West Africa, including female ancestors, female gods and elderly women.

Gelede takes the form of drama, dance and song. Selected men dress up as women and stand on long stilts wearing brightly painted wooden masks. These performances highlight the power of maternal spirits, and the way these spirits can give rise to both good and destructive events.

WHERE AND WHEN Gelede is celebrated by the Yoruba communities in south-west Nigeria, and parts of Benin and Togo every year. It takes place at the end of the harvest in the dry season, between March and May. It can also be performed in times of hardship, such as at funerals or during epidemics.

Gelede performances contain moral messages to strengthen community bonds. They also remind villagers about how they managed to endure and overcome hardships in the past.

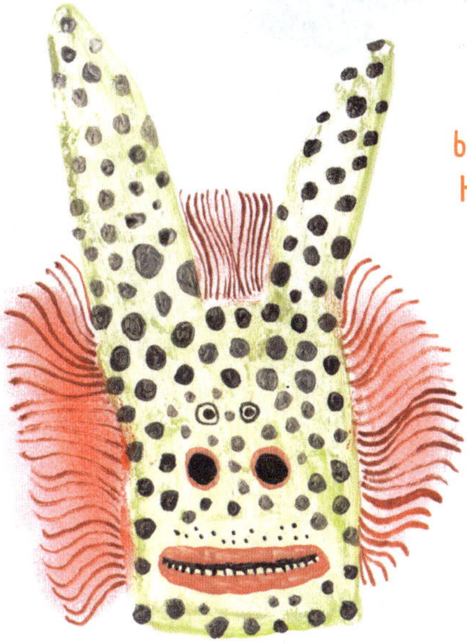

The skill of mask making is a closely guarded secret because masks are thought to hold special power to control and influence people.

Gelede performers wear a colourful headdress or mask that extends to the top of the head, sometimes featuring carved figures or a scene. Throughout Africa, masks are used to convey important messages to people through fun and entertainment, playing a powerful role in maintaining social values and social cohesion.

The figurehead for Gelede is the mother goddess Iyà Nlà.

Gelede performances are designed to remind villagers to honour and appease the almighty power of maternal spirits to keep the spirits calm, wise and healing. Yoruba people believe the spirits can ward off evil forces of witchcraft, which they believe can cause life-threatening disasters like epidemics, conflicts or drought.

Ige hopes the Gelede festival will please the female gods so that they bring enough rain to grow food for everyone in the village.

HALLOWE'EN

GO TRICK-OR-TREATING ON THE SPOOKIEST NIGHT OF THE YEAR

Today, Hallowe'en is seen as a fun day to wear costumes, go trick-or-treating, carve jack-o'-lanterns and eat sweet treats, however its roots are a much darker mix of early Christian festivals and ancient pagan rituals.

Pagan influences on Hallowe'en are thought to originate from the ancient Celtic festival of Samhain, which marked the end of the summer harvest season in Ireland and other parts of the UK and Europe. During Samhain, it was believed that the door to the 'other world' was open, making it easier for the souls of the dead to return. Celts would try to distance themselves from evil spirits by disguising themselves, lighting bonfires, or making offerings of food to get on the souls' good sides.

Over time, Christians incorporated some of the traditions of Samhain into their own celebrations on All Hallows' Evening (31 October), which they believed was the last chance for bad spirits to bring vengeance on the living. By dressing up in scary costumes, Christians believed they could hide among the spirits and trick them, warding off any danger they might bring.

WHERE AND WHEN Hallowe'en takes place on 31 October every year in the United States, Canada, Ireland, the UK and many other countries.

While today's trick-or-treaters dress up in scary costumes and call at houses with the threat of pranks if they are not given sweets, early Christians would go from door to door to receive 'soul cakes'. In return, they would pray for the souls of those in the household.

Jade carves a jack-o'-lantern to decorate the window of her house. Spiders' webs, bats and skeletons decorate her neighbours' houses.

Pumpkins are turned into jack-o'-lanterns, with carved-out faces and candles lighting them from inside. These decorations refer to an Irish story about a cheating man called Jack O'Lantern, who was rejected from both heaven and hell after tricking the devil. After his trick backfired, Jack was doomed to roam the earth with a turnip lamp, illuminated by a piece of burning coal from hell.

Trick-or-treating is a modern-day version of an early Christian practice called 'souling'.

HANUKKAH

LIGHT EIGHT CANDLES FOR EIGHT DAYS AND NIGHTS IN JUDAISM'S FESTIVAL OF LIGHTS

Hanukkah, sometimes spelled Chanukah, is a joyous Jewish festival with special holiday songs, games, food and presents. The celebration lasts for eight days and eight nights, commemorating the 'miracle of light' that helped Judeans overthrow their oppressors, the Seleucids, and reclaim the Jewish temple in Judea (now known as Jerusalem) in the year 164.

One of Judaism's holy texts, the *Talmud*, describes how the Seleucids left only enough oil in the temple to light the candelabrum for one day. Despite this, the oil burned for eight days, giving the Judeans more time to secure their place there. The longevity of the burning oil is seen as a miracle performed by God to help Judeans re-establish the Jewish faith. Hanukkah (which means 'dedication') commemorates this event with the burning of oil, now a modern-day symbol of the victory of light over darkness.

WHERE AND WHEN Hanukkah is celebrated in Israel and many other places in the world with Jewish communities. Hanukkah lasts for eight days and nights from the 25th day of Kislev (the ninth month of the Hebrew calendar), which falls in late November to mid-December each year.

Each night, for eight nights, a candle is lit in a *menorah* (a special candelabrum) while people recite blessings and prayers. The light from the *menorah* symbolises the miracle of the burning oil and the Jewish people's faith in the presence of God's light to guide them.

After the sun sets, Adam places the *menorah* in the front window of his house so that people passing by can see the lights and remember the miracle of Hanukkah.

Deep-fried food, such as *sufganiyot* (jam donuts sprinkled with icing sugar) and *latke* (potato pancakes), is traditionally eaten during Hanukkah to commemorate the miracle of the oil that burnt for eight days.

Religious ceremonies are held by rabbis (religious leaders) in synagogues, where different parts of the *Torah* (the Jewish scripture) are read aloud.

Children play with a dreidel, a four-sided spinning top with a Hebrew letter on each side.

HOLI

THROW PAINT AND HAVE A BALL AT INDIA'S SPRING FESTIVAL OF COLOUR

The arrival of spring, with its promise of colour and new life, is celebrated vividly during India's Holi festival. The festival begins on the evening known as Holika Dahan, followed by Rangwali Holi the next day. Friends, families and strangers gather from early morning to throw sacks of coloured powder, flower petals and water balloons with joyous abandon. The air becomes thick with a kaleidoscope of colour and a sense of merriment and chaos pervades the streets as people dance, party and eat festival delicacies.

WHERE AND WHEN Holi lasts for a night and a day throughout India, starting on the evening of the full moon between late February and late March each year. It has special significance in cities associated with Lord Krishna, such as Mathura in Uttar Pradesh, but it also occurs in other countries with Hindu populations, including Bangladesh, Pakistan, Suriname, South Africa and Malaysia.

Holi is a time to forgive past errors and forget past conflicts.

Holi is a Hindu tradition that dates back almost 1500 years in celebration of the triumph of good over evil, when the Lord Vishnu burned the demoness Holika.

On the evening of Rangwali Holi family and friends gather together to embrace, exchange sweets and wish each other good luck for the year ahead.

Treats including *gujiya* – a sweet dumpling filled with dried fruit, nuts and cardamom – are prepared across India.

Saanvi and Davaj stay up late on the night known as Holika Dahan to watch the large bonfire, which commemorates the burning of the demoness Holika.

Rangwali Holi includes everyone! In the streets, the joyful chaos and clouds of colour erase social barriers, uniting rich and poor, young and old, and bringing strangers together.

The colour red symbolises love, fertility and matrimony. The colour blue represents Krishna. The colour green represents new beginnings.

KONAKI SUMO

BLOCK YOUR EARS AT THE JAPANESE CRYING BABY FESTIVAL KNOWN AS THE 'SUMO OF TEARS'

Who said a screaming baby should be avoided at all costs? According to Japanese tradition, crying babies bring blessings of good health from the gods! This is the basis of Konaki Sumo, a 400-year-old Shinto tradition held in temples throughout Japan.

Two enormous scary-looking Sumo wrestlers compete to see who can be the first to make a baby cry. They each hold a baby, facing one another, while on the sidelines a priest shouts and waves at the babies, ordering them to *nake, nake* (cry, cry). The baby who cries first wins, because it is believed that a *konaki* (crying) baby grows fast, and receives good health and blessings from God. If both babies start crying at the same time the winner is the baby who cries the loudest. In fact, the louder an infant wails, the more blessed it is by the gods.

WHERE AND WHEN The Konaki Sumo is held in various temples across Japan at different times throughout the year. It is held every April in the Sensoji Temple in Tokyo, with around 100 babies.

Sometimes the babies end up laughing! At that point the wrestlers make ferocious growling faces, which usually do the trick.

Misaki lines up with hundreds of mothers to have her baby, Akari, blessed in the Konaki Sumo ceremony.

The babies are held aloft so that their tears are blessed.

The face-off between Sumo wrestlers is not usually so gentle! While sumo wrestling is now commonly known as Japan's national sport, it was first performed as a Shinto ritual to honour the spirits, essences or gods known as *kami*. *Kami* take the form of things or concepts important to life, such as wind, rain, mountains, trees, rivers and fertility.

Konaki Sumo is an important time for Japanese families to pray for their babies' health. Demons or evil spirits are said to be driven away by the wailing babies, which is why so many mothers line up, infants in arms, to enter this competition.

KUMBH MELA

TAKE A HOLY DIP AT THE LARGEST BATHING FESTIVAL ON THE PLANET

Young and old, rich and poor, Hindu and non-Hindu – all are welcome to join in the largest peaceful gathering of humans on the planet. Kumbh Mela is an ancient mass bathing ritual celebrated four times over twelve years, the largest taking place in India's holy city of Prayag at the meeting of three rivers: the Ganges, the Yamuna and the Saraswati. Millions of devout Hindus take the plunge into holy rivers to wash away their wrongdoings and escape the cycle of death and rebirth.

WHERE AND WHEN The biggest Kumbh Mela happens every twelve years in Prayag, Allahabad, over a six-week period in January and February. There are also three other minor Kumbh Melas celebrated once every three years in Haridwar (on the Ganges River), Ujjain (on the Shipra River) and Nashik (on the Godavari River).

Ananya takes a dip in the sacred → river at Prayag; she believes this holy water will wash away her sins and help her reach immortality.

The Kumbh Mela festival in Allahabad attracts up to 150 million pilgrims.

Kumbh Mela is sometimes referred to as the 'festival of the sacred pitcher'. According to ancient mythology, the Hindu god Vishnu was carrying a *kumbh* (pot) containing the precious nectar of immortality when he spilled four drops of it during a twelve-day struggle between the gods and demons. These drops spilt into four different places, which are now the locations of the four Kumbh Melas that take place over a twelve-year period.

Processions of *sadhus* (holy men) riding in chariots and on the backs of elephants and horses mark the beginning of Kumbh Mela.

Sadhus and *sadhvis* (holy women) bathe in the holy rivers. These are people who give up all material comforts and worldly pleasures to prove their devotion to Lord Vishnu.

LA TOMATINA

GET SPLATTERED AT SPAIN'S MAD AND MESSY TOMATO-THROWING PARTY

Have you ever been told not to play with your food? Well no one is going to stop you if you head to Buñol in Spain for their tomato-throwing festival!

La Tomatina is the world's largest food fight. The frenzy begins when a dozen trucks dump loads of tomatoes in the town's cramped main square. Many thousands of people pelt tomatoes at each other for an hour, turning them into a thick red juice, completely covering everyone from head to toe.

How and why did La Tomatina start? One theory is that it emerged from a street brawl in 1945, when one rowdy local started throwing vegetables at people in a street parade. Some young people retaliated and a huge food fight broke out. The following year the same people picked a fight on purpose and brought their own supply of tomatoes!

WHERE AND WHEN La Tomatina takes place in the tiny Spanish town of Buñol in the province of Valencia, usually on the last Saturday in August.

Due to La Tomatina's huge popularity, the number of participants has been limited to just 20 000 lucky ticketholders.

Any volunteers to clean up the mess? Firefighters arrive to hose down the streets – and people – after the battle.

La Tomatina has one rule: participants must crush the tomatoes before throwing them. Being hit by a tomato can hurt!

Around 150 000 over-ripe tomatoes are splattered within one hour!

La Tomatina was banned when Francisco Franco ruled Spain because it had no religious significance. The tradition was revived again in the 1970s.

Tomatoes contain natural disinfectant due to their high levels of acidity, so any small injuries will stay relatively clean.

LUNAR NEW YEAR

PILE ONTO BUSES, TRAINS AND PLANES TO BE WITH FAMILY FOR ONE OF THE WORLD'S BIGGEST NEW YEAR CELEBRATIONS

Lunar New Year, also known as Chinese New Year or Spring Festival, is the biggest and most important celebration in China and many other countries throughout Asia. The number of people who travel across China or internationally to spend the New Year with family is one of the largest annual human migrations on the planet!

In China, celebrations begin on New Year's Eve, when people gather to eat dumplings after midnight in a traditional dinner called *Nian Ye Fan*. Festivities usually last for around fifteen days leading up to a large street parade, called the Lantern Festival. Red lanterns decorate the streets and people dressed in red enjoy music, parades, acrobatics and traditional dances. A giant dancing dragon weaves through the streets, symbolising strength, wisdom, power and wealth.

WHERE AND WHEN Lunar New Year is celebrated in many countries throughout Asia and across the world. It marks the beginning of the first month in the Chinese (lunisolar) calendar, which falls at the end of January or the beginning of February each year.

Each Lunar New Year is represented by one of the twelve Chinese zodiac signs.

Red lanterns are hung everywhere in China, symbolising the return of light, the coming of spring and the beginning of the new growing season.

Salt-cured fish hang in the streets of China. Fish symbolises prosperity and is often eaten during the Lunar New Year celebrations.

In China the colour red symbolises good fortune and happiness. Red is also thought to scare away the lion monster, Nian, in preparation for a happy new year.

The Dragon Dance is performed to scare away evil spirits and to bring good luck in the New Year.

The giant dragon weaves through the streets to the sound of cymbals, a gong and a big drum, held up by performers standing underneath.

In Beijing, Zhang Li enjoys a midnight feast of dumplings, called *jiaozi*. A coin is hidden inside one of the dumplings. If she finds the coin, it is believed she will have good luck for the rest of the year!

MATARIKI

FLY KITES AS YOU WAIT FOR A CLUSTER OF STARS TO TWINKLE IN THE MIDWINTER SKY

The rising of the star cluster 'Matariki' in New Zealand's midwinter sky has always been an important event for Māori people. Traditionally, it marked a time for remembering the dead, a time for celebrating new life and a guide for planning the new year ahead.

The appearance of Matariki (otherwise known as the Pleiades star cluster, or the 'Seven Sisters') predicted the environment and conditions of the coming year. If Matariki appeared bright and clear, there would be a good growing season and lots of fish and birds to eat. If the stars appeared hazy or closely bunched together, a cold winter was in store and planting was put off until October. This knowledge was considered vital for survival.

Matariki was also a time to remember those who had passed away in the previous year. Māori believed the stars carried the souls of the ancestors, their spirits released into the sky. Although this was a sad time for many, it also marked the new year ahead.

Matariki traditionally happened at the end of harvest and, with food aplenty, Māori celebrated! Women sang and danced to welcome the change of season and new beginnings. And to get close to the stars some flew *pākau* (kites) from the hilltops. However, Matariki celebrations began to dwindle after Europeans colonised New Zealand in 1840, leaving Māori traditions sidelined right up until the 1970s.

In recent years, Matariki has enjoyed a resurgence in popularity, culminating in diverse festivals and events celebrated by all New Zealanders.

WHERE AND WHEN Matariki events take place throughout New Zealand. The date changes every year, depending on the first appearance of the stars or the new moon, any time between late May and July.

← Mika gets up before sunset to see the stars rise on the north-east horizon.

The stars carry the souls of ancestors, guiding the living into the new year ahead.

Today, families gather together, share food, make paper stars and fly kites. In the evening, there's singing and dancing as fireworks light up the sky to mark the yearly event.

WHIRLING DERVISHES FESTIVAL

WATCH WHITE ROBES SPIN IN A MYSTICAL SUFI CEREMONY IN TURKEY

In the Turkish town of Konya, a spellbinding form of ritual prayer becomes a mesmerising occasion for a week each December. Devotees of the Sufi Mevlevî Order gather to spin on one foot for long periods of time, dressed in white capes and long white robes that rise up into hypnotic spinning discs. These 'whirling dervishes', as they are called, spin as a form of worship, marking their devotion to Allah, while honouring a Sufi mystic, poet and Islamic religious figure known as 'Mevlânâ' or 'Rūmī' (short for Jalāl ad-Dīn Muhammad Rūmī). Rūmī inspired the Mevlevî Order and started whirling as a form of religious meditation and worship around 750 years ago. The Mevlevî Order is part of Sufism, which focuses on the mystical elements within Islam.

The last day of the festival is the highlight, commemorating Rūmī's death in Konya in 1273. This day is often referred to as Rūmī's wedding night, since it is believed that it was upon his death that he entered into union with Allah.

The *Sema*, the worship ceremony, begins with the removal of black cloaks, symbolising the dervishes' readiness to be spiritually reborn in white. With each 360-degree turn, the word 'Allāh' is chanted in-between rhythmical breathing. The dervishes gradually twirl faster and faster, leading into a trance-like state, where they become a conduit for divine blessings. They raise both arms to the sky, with the right palm pointing upwards to receive God's grace, and the left palm pointing downwards to channel this grace back to Earth. They wear brown cylindrical hats that symbolise an openness to communion with God.

WHERE AND WHEN The Whirling Dervishes Festival occurs in Konya, Turkey, between 10 and 17 December each year.

The Sufi mystic Rūmī is one of Iran and Turkey's most famous poets, and is revered throughout the world. Rūmī's tombstone in Konya attracts tens of thousands of visitors each year.

Baris practises the flute in the hope of one day accompanying the musicians who play at the *Sema*.

Whirling dervishes spin around and around as a form of worship.

SEASONAL FESTIVALS: SPRING

NOWRUZ

HANG YOUR RUGS OUTSIDE IN IRAN'S BIG SPRING-CLEANING HOLIDAY

Nowruz is the most significant holiday in the Iranian calendar, marking the first day of spring and the first day of the new year. The holiday lasts for 13 days, during which Iranian families spend time spring-cleaning their houses, celebrating with gifts and food and visiting the home of their oldest family member.

The origins of Nowruz lie in Zoroastrianism, an ancient Persian religion practised more than 3000 years ago in the vast territories of the former Persian Empires that extended beyond the borders of modern-day Iran. This is why millions of non-Iranian people in diverse parts of the world celebrate Nowruz today.

Nowruz is celebrated on the day of the vernal equinox, usually on or around 21 March. It is observed in the Balkans, the Black Sea Basin, the Caucasus, many parts of Asia, the Middle East and other regions.

Bahar lights a candle on a ceremonial *haftseen* table containing a collection of seven foods that symbolise renewal and hope for the new year. Dried fruit, apples, garlic, sprouts, sweet pudding, vinegar and the Persian spice sumac represent qualities like love, beauty and health, medicine and well-being, rebirth and renewal, wealth and fertility, patience and wisdom, and the sunrise of a new day.

Sprouts

Apples

Sumac

Dried fruit

Pudding

Vinegar

Garlic

HANAMI

SEE JAPAN'S CHERRY BLOSSOM TREES IN FULL BLOOM

Spring heralds the blooming of cherry blossom trees in Japan, and people throughout the country flock to gardens and parks to celebrate. *Hanami* (viewing flowers) is a tradition dating back more than 1000 years to a time when aristocrats enjoyed looking at beautiful cherry blossoms and wrote poems inspired by them. Today, people enjoy the blooming of *sakura* (cherry blossoms) and sometimes *ume* (plum blossoms) by picnicking in parks or in the countryside. Ueno Park in Tokyo is particularly famous for its avenue of cherry blossoms festooned with over 1000 lanterns lit up at night.

Cherry blossom season is late March or early April. It can be earlier or later in other parts of Japan, depending on the region's weather.

SEASONAL FESTIVALS: SUMMER

ABU SIMBEL SUN FESTIVAL

BEHOLD ANCIENT EGYPT'S HOMAGE TO THE SUN AT RAMESES II'S GREAT TEMPLE

Egypt is one of the hottest, driest and sunniest countries in the world, so it is not surprising that the most important god for ancient Egyptians was the god of the sun, known as Ra or Re. Ra was the giver of light and life to the cosmos, and he was often associated with another god, Amun, becoming Amun-Ra, the sun god king.

The Sun Festival is an ancient event dedicated to the appearance of the sun at the Great Temple at Abu Simbel. The temple was built around 13 BCE by the powerful Egyptian king Rameses II in honour of the sun gods and of himself. The temple lives in darkness all through the year except for two days (22 February and 22 October) when the central chamber of the temple is lit up by the sun. For a short period of time, the sun aligns perfectly to illuminate the temple's inner statues of Ra and Amun-Ra, leaving Ptah, the god of the underworld, in darkness.

Rashida arrives at the temple early to see the sun rise and cut through the darkness of the temple's inner chamber. Afterwards, she watches a traditional Nubian dance while eating a pasta, rice and lentil dish, called *koshari*.

MIDSOMMAR

PICNIC IN A PARK ON SWEDEN'S MOST LIGHT-FILLED DAY OF THE YEAR

Midsommar (or the summer solstice) is the longest and lightest day of the year, when the sun reaches its highest point in the sky. After a long, dark and cold winter, the longest day is a time of great joy in Sweden, with families and friends decorating their houses with flowers, and flocking to parks and gardens to picnic on traditional foods such as pickled herring, cured salmon and new potatoes, while sipping flavoured schnapps, beer and spiced vodka. A traditional maypole covered in greenery is raised, with people dressed in handmade costumes, with crowns fashioned from wildflowers and birch, singing and dancing around it. The celebrations can last for days, beginning around the third Friday and Saturday in June.

Erik visits Stockholm's open-air Skansen museum to see the dancing around the maypole.

SEASONAL FESTIVALS: AUTUMN

THANKSGIVING DAY

FEAST WITH FAMILY AND FRIENDS, AND GIVE THANKS FOR NATURE'S BOUNTY

Thanksgiving is a time for Americans and Canadians to celebrate the previous year's fortunes with an elaborate family dinner. Typical American dishes are enjoyed, such as turkey, potatoes, squash, corn, green beans, cranberries and pumpkin pie.

Thanksgiving originated as an autumn harvest festival, when early Americans gathered together to enjoy a large feast before the arrival of winter. This was an opportunity for Christians to thank God for their yield of bountiful crops. Some historians suggest that the earliest Thanksgiving celebration in the United States dates back to 1621, when colonial pilgrims shared their first harvest meal in Plymouth with the Wampanoag people (the local Indigenous American people). Today, Thanksgiving is a public holiday throughout America celebrated by Christians and non-Christians alike.

Thanksgiving is celebrated on the fourth Thursday of November in the United States and Brazil, and the second Monday of October in Canada. It is also celebrated in the Caribbean islands and Liberia.

Lillith uses her grandmother's recipe to bake a pumpkin pie.

FULL MOON FESTIVAL

CELEBRATE THE MOON'S LIFE-FORCE WITH MOONCAKES UNDER THE LIGHT OF THE FULL MOON

The Full Moon Festival is celebrated in China and Vietnam in the middle of autumn on a full moon evening. Dating back thousands of years, it was traditionally celebrated to honour the power and life-giving properties of the moon during harvest time. Ancient Chinese emperors saw that the movement of the moon had a close relationship with seasonal changes, affecting the growth of foods such as rice and wheat.

Nowadays, the Full Moon Festival is a time to reunite with family and friends. When the full moon rises, friends and relatives gather to watch, while eating mooncakes (a dense pastry filled with sweet-bean or lotus-seed paste) and sing moon poems together. Incense is also burned in temples to honour ancestors and the moon goddess of immortality, called Chang'e.

The festival falls on the 15th day of the eighth lunar month across China and Vietnam (usually in September or October each year). Celebrations also occur in many other countries influenced by Chinese culture, especially in East Asia.

Bai watches a lion dance, before watching brightly coloured lanterns floating in the sky and hanging from towers ⟵ and poles.

SEASONAL FESTIVALS: WINTER

THORRABLOT

EAT, DRINK AND BE MERRY DURING ICELAND'S BIGGEST MIDWINTER FEAST

As winter reaches its darkest and coldest month in Iceland, people come together for one night to celebrate Thorrablot, a midwinter feast of traditional Icelandic delicacies.

Dating back more than a thousand years to the time of the Vikings, Thorrablot was originally practised as a sacrificial midwinter offering to the Norse god Thor. Communal feasting on the meat of sacrificed animals was practised to ensure fertility and growth in the new year. Today, Icelanders serve what was once everyday food for Vikings, so it is not uncommon to find fermented shark meat, boiled sheep's head, or congealed sheep's blood wrapped in a ram's stomach on offer! Traditional songs, dancing, games, storytelling and poetry continue until the early hours of the morning. Thorrablot usually takes place on the first Friday after 19 January.

Gunnar eats blood pudding with his family, which is made out of lamb blood and suet (the raw hard fat of beef or mutton) mixed with rye and oats. His sister, Arnkatla, looks forward to her favourite dish: seal's flippers cured in lactic acid.

GROUNDHOG DAY

OBSERVE THE SHADOW OF A GROUNDHOG IN ONE OF NORTH AMERICA'S STRANGEST WINTER TRADITIONS

Towards the end of winter, Americans and Canadians wait expectantly for a large, furry groundhog to emerge from its burrow underground. The groundhog's shadow is thought to predict the length of winter. If the groundhog's shadow is long (due to a clear and sunny day) the groundhog will retreat to its den and winter will continue for at least six weeks. However, if no shadow is visible (due to a cloudy or overcast day) warm weather is expected to arrive soon, bringing an end to winter.

Groundhog Day was brought to Pennsylvania in the late 1800s by German settlers who practised the tradition on what was known as 'Candlemas Day' in Germany – a Christian tradition marking the midpoint between the winter solstice and the spring equinox. Germans typically used a badger to predict the length of winter.

Eleanor sees a long shadow cast by the emerging groundhog – spring is coming! She leaves her hat, scarf and mittens by the door. ⟶

Groundhog Day takes place on 2 February in Pennsylvania and throughout the US and Canada.

REMARKABLE REGIONAL FESTIVALS

Bali's Pakul Sapu celebrates friendships by beating each other with brooms

The Balinese villages of Mamala and Morella have an unusual way of commemorating very old friendships. The celebration is called Pakul Sapu and each year, a week after Ramadan, bare-chested men from both villages gather together to beat each other with homemade rattan or brushwood sticks until they bleed. The ritual is said to date back 400 years, to when both villages were united by their resistance to, and imprisonment by, Dutch colonists in the mid-1600s. On being released from prison, members of both villages danced, sang and beat each other with sticks. The blood from the beatings marks their mutual suffering and shared bonds.

Honour good health in Taiwan's grand Parade of the God of Medicine

The Parade of the God of Medicine commemorates the birthday of a doctor who is said to have performed medical miracles before ascending to heaven as a revered god: Emperor Baosheng Dadi. In Taipai and Hseuhchia, icons of the god and associated legendary figures are paraded through the streets on floats decorated with flowers. The procession is led by a group of priests, dancers and pilgrims (called the Centipedes) who are believed to hold special powers to banish evil spirits. Followers of the procession sometimes throw themselves in front of the Centipedes to be trampled upon, believing that this will guarantee their future good health.

The parade, sometimes called the Baosheng Cultural Festival, happens on the 14th or 15th day of the third lunar month, usually in April.

See the crowning of a goat as king in one of Ireland's oldest festivals: Puck Fair

Each August in the small Irish town of Killorglin, a goat-catcher heads into the mountains to catch a wild male goat, which will be crowned king of the town for three days and nights. The goat is paraded through the town and crowned by the Queen of Puck (a young girl, aged ten or eleven, who has won the honour by writing an outstanding essay). On the second day, King Puck is the centrepiece of a large town fair, with dancing and entertainment, before his crown is removed and he is returned to the mountains on the final day. Puck Fair is one of Ireland's oldest festivals, and many believe it has ancient pagan origins, with the male goat symbolising fertility at harvest time.

Marvel at Spain's tallest human towers during Barcelona's La Mercè festival

La Mercè officially began in 1871 as a celebration of Catalan culture and today it includes hundreds of events over four days in September. One of the highlights is a spectacular but dangerous event involving tall towers of people, sometimes standing up to 12 metres high. The construction of human *castells* (castles) began as a competition between rival groups in the 18th century. Today, a *castell* is considered successful if it can be erected and dismantled without any falls or injuries. The *castellers* chosen to climb to the top are usually children (sometimes as young as five) because they are light and nimble. When they reach the top they give a little wave to show they have completed their mission!

REMARKABLE REGIONAL FESTIVALS

Behold the floating lights at Yi Peng and Loi Krathong's festival of lanterns in Thailand

Two Thai festivals, Yi Peng and Loi Krathong, are different traditions that are nevertheless closely related. They both draw on Hinduism, but Yi Peng also draws on Buddhism. In both festivals, floating lights are released, to symbolise the letting go of negative thoughts, to express gratitude and to wish for good fortune. Both festivals are also celebrated in Chiang Mai simultaneously, around the full moon in November.

Loi Krathong also occurs at various points along the Ping River. People float candle-lit lanterns on the water inside banana leaf boats decorated with flowers and incense. The floating baskets of light thank the Buddhist goddess of water – Phra Mae Khongkha – for the fortune of having enough water, and to ask her for her forgiveness for polluting the environment.

Yi Peng only occurs in Northern Thailand. Thousands of candle-lit paper lanterns are released into the night sky after music, entertainment and prayer. Steeped in Buddhist and Hindu traditions, the lanterns symbolise wishes for renewal.

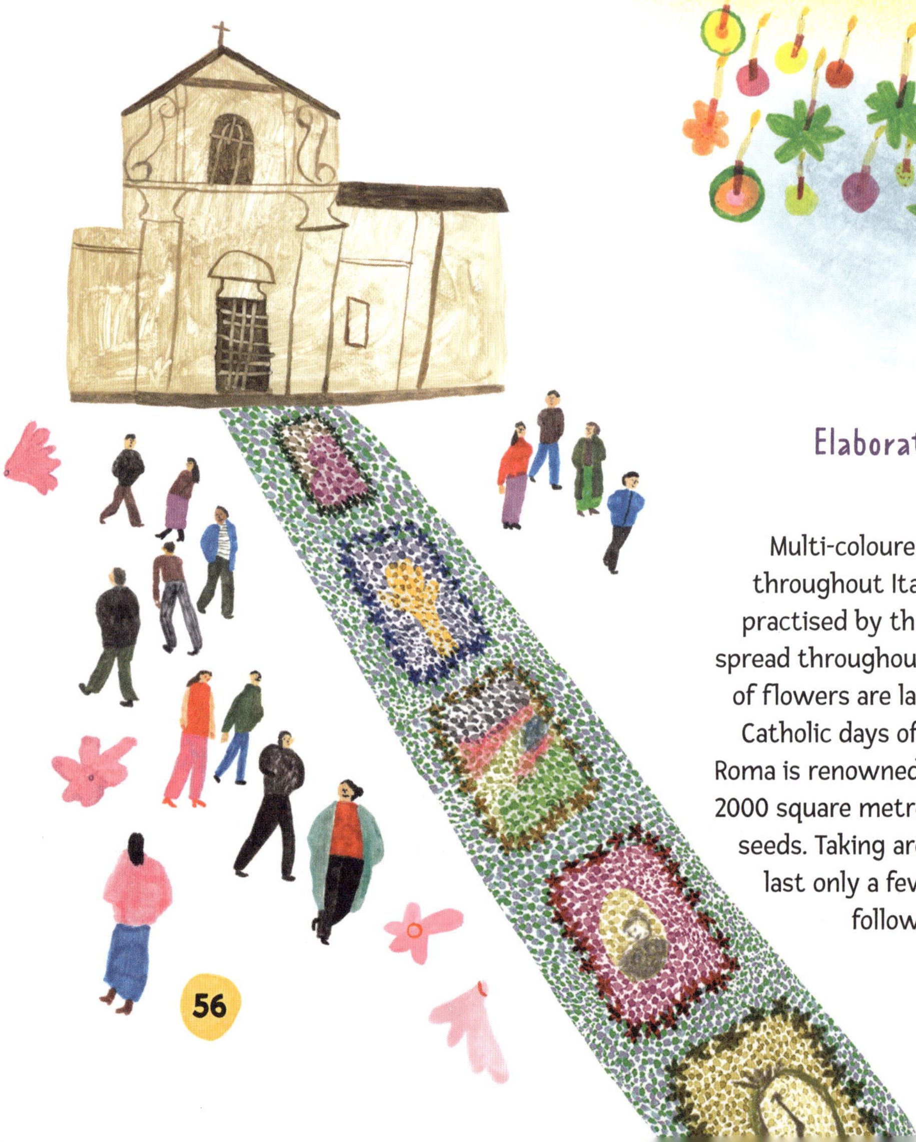

Elaborate carpets of flowers fill the streets at Infiorata in Italy

Multi-coloured artworks and mosaics made of flowers bloom throughout Italy during the religious tradition of Infiorata. First practised by the Vatican in 17th-century Rome, the tradition soon spread throughout Italy's villages and towns. Today, incredible carpets of flowers are laid on streets leading up to churches and abbeys on Catholic days of worship in May and June. The town of Genzano di Roma is renowned for its enormous carpet of flowers covering around 2000 square metres, filled with hundreds of thousands of flowers and seeds. Taking around three days to construct, the delicate carpets last only a few hours, before religious processions, sometimes followed by playful children, march over them!

Honour the sun god Inti during the Peruvian winter solstice festival, Inti Raymi

During the Inca Empire between the 14th and 15th centuries, Inti Raymi was the greatest festival of the year! Around 25 000 people gathered in the town of Cusco, Peru, to honour the sun god, Inti, who was venerated as the source of all life. Processions, dances and cloth-bound mummies – paraded from nearby temples and shrines – marked the winter solstice and the Inca New Year. Up to 200 llamas were sacrificed to entice the gods to bring a good harvest season. Today, some of the Inti Raymi festivities continue at the ancient ruins of Sacsayhuamán near Cusco, beginning on 24 June. Parades, fairs and sounds of panpipes, flutes and drums fill the streets. Traditional costumes are worn, including the dramatic *aya huma* mask with twelve horns respresenting each month of the year.

Celebrate Boxing Day and New Year's Day Junkanoo style in the Bahamas

Junkanoo began hundreds of years ago as an affirmation of African culture, when plantation slaves in the Bahamas celebrated their two days' of annual leave with a party that reminded them of their African roots and affirmed their resistance to slavery. The celebration grew into a vibrant street parade filled with bright costumes, African masks and a distinctive style of music influenced by Caribbean culture, African rhythms and American blues. Today, goatskin drums, trumpets, accordions, cowbells and whistles are the instruments played at Junkanoo, along with handsaws, which are a unique part of the distinctive Caribbean 'Rake-and-Scrape' style of music. Junkanoo is a carnival-style festival celebrated in towns across the Bahamas every Boxing Day and New Year's Day.

MARITA BULLOCK loves learning about different people and cultures, and their diverse ways of seeing and living in the world. She has taught cultural studies and literature in universities, colleges and schools across Sydney. Together with Joan-Maree, Marita runs a creative production house called Three Peaks Studio.

JOAN-MAREE HARGREAVES is inspired by the curiosity of children. She has been the editor of a number of Australian and international children's magazines, including *National Geographic Kids* and *K-Zone*. Together with Marita, Joan-Maree runs a creative production house called Three Peaks Studio.

LIZ ROWLAND is inspired by colour and pattern, and by people and cultures, and explores our interactions with each other and our environment. Her work is hand rendered using a combination of gouache, watercolour, oil and pastels.